Learn Korean for Beginners

Basic Korean Simplified for You

Written By: Ji-young S.

Published By: My First Picture Book Inc.

Copyright: My First Picture Book Inc. © 2023 · All Rights Reserved

Table of Contents

Chapter 1: Introduction to Korean Language 1

Chapter 2: Alphabet and Pronunciation 3

Chapter 3: Greetings and Basic Conversation 9

Chapter 4: Numbers and Counting 13

Chapter 5: Korean Grammar Basics 17

Chapter 6: Adjectives and Adverbs 21

Chapter 7: Verbs and Tenses 25

Chapter 8: Nouns and Articles 30

Chapter 9: Questions and Negation 34

Chapter 10: Korean Honorifics 38

Chapter 11: Korean Vocabulary 42

    Family vocabulary: 42

    Time vocabulary: 44

    Colors vocabulary: 45

    Weather vocabulary: 46

    Animals vocabulary: 47

    Transportation vocabulary: 48

    Food vocabulary: 49

    Clothing vocabulary: 50

    Emotions vocabulary: 51

Chapter 12: Korean Idioms and Expressions 52

Chapter 13: Korean Culture and Etiquette 55

Chapter 14: Korean Writing System 59

Chapter 15: Korean Slang and Colloquialisms 63

Chapter 1: Introduction to Korean Language

Korean is the official language of both North and South Korea and is also spoken by communities of Korean immigrants around the world. It is a complex language with a unique alphabet system, grammar structure, and vocabulary.

Korean language has a long history dating back to the 15th century, and it has undergone significant changes and evolution over time. The modern Korean language has been heavily influenced by Chinese, Japanese, and English languages.

The Korean alphabet, known as Hangul, was created in the 15th century by King Sejong the Great. Hangul consists of 24 letters, including 14 consonants and 10 vowels, and is designed to be easy to learn and use.

Korean is a subject-object-verb (SOV) language, which means that the subject of a sentence comes first, followed by the object, and then the verb. Korean also has a complex honorific system, which is used to show respect and politeness to people of higher social status.

Here are some important features of the Korean Language:

1. Vocabulary: Korean vocabulary is derived from various sources such as Chinese characters, English, Japanese, and native Korean words. The language has a large number of homophones, which can sometimes make it difficult for learners to distinguish between similar-sounding words.

2. Politeness: As mentioned earlier, Korean has a complex honorific system, which is used to show respect and politeness to people of higher social status. This system affects not only verbs but also pronouns, nouns, and adjectives.

3. Pronunciation: Korean pronunciation can also be a bit challenging for non-native speakers. The language has several unique sounds, such as the aspirated consonants and tense vowels. The pitch accent also plays an important role in Korean, as changing the pitch of a word can completely alter its meaning.

4. Grammar: Korean grammar is different from English and many other languages. The SOV structure, where the verb comes at the end of the sentence, can be confusing for beginners. Korean also uses particles to indicate the subject, object, and topic of a sentence.

5. Culture: Learning Korean can provide you with a deeper understanding of Korean culture, including its history, art, music, and cuisine. Korean popular culture, such as K-dramas and K-pop, has gained worldwide popularity in recent years, making learning Korean more relevant than ever.

Korean language learning can be a challenging yet rewarding experience, but with dedicated practice and a good learning plan, anyone can become proficient in the language. Learning Korean can provide access to Korean culture, media, and business opportunities, as well as connect you to a vibrant and diverse global community.

Chapter 2: Alphabet and Pronunciation

Alphabet in Korean Language:

The Korean writing system consists of 24 basic letters, which are known as jamo. These 24 jamo can be combined to form all the syllables used in the Korean language. The 24 jamo are further divided into two categories: vowels and consonants.

1. Vowels: There are 10 basic vowels in Korean language. They are:

    - ㅏ (a)
    - ㅓ (eo)
    - ㅗ (o)
    - ㅜ (u)
    - ㅡ (eu)
    - ㅣ (i)
    - ㅐ (ae)
    - ㅔ (e)
    - ㅚ (oe)
    - ㅟ (wi)

2. Consonants: There are 14 basic consonants in Korean language. They are:

    - ㄱ (g/k)
    - ㄴ (n)
    - ㄷ (d/t)

- ㄹ (r/l)
- ㅁ (m)
- ㅂ (b/p)
- ㅅ (s)
- ㅇ (ng)
- ㅈ (j/ch)
- ㅊ (ch)
- ㅋ (k)
- ㅌ (t)
- ㅍ (p)
- ㅎ (h)

Pronunciation in Korean Language:

Korean pronunciation can be challenging for English speakers because it has some sounds that are not used in English. It is important to note that the pronunciation of a Korean letter may vary depending on its position within a syllable.

1. Vowels: Korean vowels are pronounced more sharply than English vowels. The pronunciation of each vowel is as follows:

   - ㅏ (a) - similar to the "a" in "father"
   - ㅓ (eo) - similar to the "eo" in "sister"
   - ㅗ (o) - similar to the "o" in "note"
   - ㅜ (u) - similar to the "u" in "put"
   - ㅡ (eu) - similar to the "u" in "book"
   - ㅣ (i) - similar to the "ee" in "feet"
   - ㅐ (ae) - similar to the "ai" in "rain"
   - ㅔ (e) - similar to the "e" in "bet"
   - ㅚ (oe) - a combination of the "o" and "e" sounds
   - ㅟ (wi) - a combination of the "u" and "i" sounds

2. Consonants: The pronunciation of Korean consonants can vary depending on their position within a syllable. Some important points to note about the pronunciation of Korean consonants are:

   - ㄱ (g/k) - When it appears at the beginning of a syllable, it is pronounced as "g." When it appears at the end of a syllable, it is pronounced as "k."
   - ㄴ (n) - Pronounced similar to the "n" in "now."
   - ㄷ (d/t) - When it appears at the beginning of a syllable, it is pronounced as "d." When it appears at the end of a syllable, it is pronounced as "t."
   - ㄹ (r/l) - Pronunciation can vary between "r" and "l" depending on its position within a word. When it appears at the beginning of a syllable or after another consonant, it is pronounced as a "r" sound, similar to the Spanish "rr" or the French "r." However, when ㄹ is at the end of a syllable or word, it is pronounced as an "l" sound. This pronunciation can vary between "r" and "l" depending on its position within a word, so it is important to pay attention to the context and surrounding sounds.
   - ㅁ (m) - Pronounced similar to the "m" in "me."
   - ㅂ (b/p) - When it appears at the beginning of a syllable, it is pronounced as "b." When it appears at the end of a syllable, it is pronounced as "p."
   - ㅅ (s) - Pronounced similar to the "s" in "sea."
   - ㅇ (ng) - Pronounced similar to the "ng" in "sing." However, when it appears at the beginning of a syllable, it is silent and simply serves as a placeholder for a vowel.
   - ㅈ (j/ch) - When it appears at the beginning of a syllable, it is pronounced as "j." When it appears at the end of a syllable, it is pronounced as "ch."
   - ㅊ (ch) - Pronounced similar to the "ch" in "chat."
   - ㅋ (k) - Pronounced similar to the "k" in "kick."
   - ㅌ (t) - Pronounced similar to the "t" in "talk."

- ㅍ (p) - Pronounced similar to the "p" in "pen."
- ㅎ (h) - Pronounced similar to the "h" in "hi."

It's worth noting that some Korean consonants have a stronger emphasis than others, and are pronounced with a stronger puff of air. These consonants are called aspirated consonants, and they include ㅋ, ㅌ, ㅍ, ㅊ, ㅎ. Aspirated consonants are pronounced with a stronger puff of air than their non-aspirated counterparts. For example, the "k" in "kick" is an aspirated consonant, while the "g" in "go" is a non-aspirated consonant.

Double Consonants and Vowels: In addition to the basic 24 letters, there are also double consonants and vowels in Korean language. Double consonants are pronounced with a stronger emphasis than their single counterparts. The double consonants in Korean are:

- ㄲ (kk)
- ㄸ (tt)
- ㅃ (pp)
- ㅆ (ss)
- ㅉ (jj)

Double vowels, on the other hand, are pronounced as a lengthened version of their single counterpart. The double vowels in Korean are:

- ㅐ (ae) → ㅒ (yae)
- ㅔ (e) → ㅖ (ye)
- ㅏ (a) → ㅑ (ya)
- ㅓ (eo) → ㅕ (yeo)
- ㅗ (o) → ㅛ (yo)
- ㅜ (u) → ㅠ (yu)

Pronunciation Rules: There are some pronunciation rules in Korean that can affect the way certain letters are pronounced. Some of these rules are:

- When the consonant ㅇ (ng) appears at the beginning of a syllable, it is not pronounced as a consonant but rather as a vowel sound similar to the English "uh" or "ng" sound.
- When the consonants ㄱ, ㄷ, ㅂ, or ㅈ appear next to each other in a word, they are pronounced as double consonants. For example, the word "밖" (bak) meaning "outside" is pronounced with a double "k" sound.
- When the consonants ㄱ, ㄷ, or ㅂ appear at the end of a syllable followed by the consonant ㅅ, they are pronounced as "k," "t," or "p" respectively. For example, the word "앞서" (apseo) meaning "before" is pronounced with a "t" sound for the ㄷ.
- When the consonants ㄹ or ㅎ appear at the end of a syllable followed by the vowel ㅇ (ng), they are pronounced as "n" and "ng" respectively. For example, the word "밤안" (bam-an) meaning "inside the night" is pronounced with an "n" sound for the ㄹ.

Accent: Korean has a tonal accent system, where the pitch of a syllable can change the meaning of a word. However, unlike some tonal languages such as Mandarin Chinese, the tonal accents in Korean are not as prominent or strictly defined. In general, the first syllable of a word is pronounced with a higher pitch than the rest of the syllables.

Pronunciation Tips: Here are some tips that can help you improve your pronunciation in Korean:

- Listen to native speakers and practice imitating their pronunciation.
- Pay attention to the length and emphasis of syllables, as well as the pitch of your voice.

- Practice pronouncing individual syllables and words slowly and accurately before attempting to speak at a faster pace.
- Use language learning resources such as audio recordings, pronunciation guides, and online tools to help you improve your pronunciation.

Common Pronunciation Mistakes: Here are some common mistakes that English speakers may make when learning Korean pronunciation:

- Pronouncing ㄹ (r/l) as an English "r" sound, when it is actually somewhere in between an "r" and an "l" sound.
- Pronouncing ㅓ (eo) and ㅗ (o) as English "e" and "o" respectively, when their sounds are actually closer to "uh" and "aw."
- Not pronouncing the double consonants and vowels correctly, which can change the meaning of a word. For example, the word "갈비" (galbi) meaning "ribs" is different from the word "갈비살" (galbisal) meaning "rib meat."

Chapter 3: Greetings and Basic Conversation

Basic Greetings:

- 안녕하세요 (annyeonghaseyo) - This is the most common and formal way of saying "hello" in Korean. It can be used in any situation, whether you're meeting someone for the first time or greeting someone older or of higher social status.

- 안녕 (annyeong) - This is a more casual and informal way of saying "hello" to someone you know well, such as a friend or family member.

- 안녕하십니까 (annyeonghasimnikka) - This is an even more formal version of "안녕하세요" and is typically used in very formal or official settings.

- 반갑습니다 (bangapseumnida) - This means "nice to meet you" and is a common phrase to use when meeting someone for the first time.

Basic Conversation:

Once you've exchanged greetings with someone, there are several common phrases and questions you can use to start a basic conversation in Korean:

- 이름이 뭐에요? (ireumi mwoeyo?) - This means "What is your name?" and is a polite way to ask someone for their name.

- 어디서 왔어요? (eodiseo wasseoyo?) - This means "Where are you from?" and is a common question to ask someone you've just met.

- 한국어를 할 수 있어요? (hangukeoreul hal su isseoyo?) - This means "Can you speak Korean?" and is a good way to start a conversation if you're unsure of the other person's language abilities.

- 뭐 좋아하세요? (mwo johaseyo?) - This means "What do you like?" and is a good way to start a conversation about hobbies or interests.

- 오늘 날씨가 좋아요 (oneul nalssiga johayo) - This means "Today's weather is good" and is a common topic of conversation, especially if you're in a new place or meeting someone for the first time.

- 음식이 맛있어요 (eumsigi masisseoyo) - This means "The food is delicious" and is a good thing to say if you're enjoying a meal with someone.

- 감사합니다 (gamsahamnida) - This means "Thank you" and is a polite way to show appreciation for something.

- 잘 지내세요 (jal jinaeseyo) - This means "Take care" and is a polite way to say goodbye or end a conversation.

Here are some more basic sentences:

- 만나서 반갑습니다. (mannaseo bangapseumnida.) - Nice to meet you.

- 저도요. (jeodo yo.) - Me too.

- 저는 한국에서 왔어요. (jeoneun hangukeseo wasseoyo.) - I'm from Korea.

- 한국어 잘 하시네요. (hangugeo jal hasineyo.) - You speak Korean well.

- 이제 어디 가실 거예요? (ije eodi gasil geoyeyo?) - Where are you going now?

- 제 친구를 만나러 가고 있어요. (je chingureul mannareo gago isseoyo.) - I'm going to meet my friend.

- 그럼 잘 가세요. (geureom jal gaseyo.) - Okay, have a good time.

- 어디에 살아요? (eodie sarayo?) - Where do you live?

- 저는 학생이에요. (jeoneun haksaengieyo.) - I am a student.

- 뭐 좀 추천해 주세요. (mwo jom chucheonhae juseyo.) – Can you recommend something?

- 이게 얼마예요? (ige eolmayeyo?) - How much is this?

- 뭐 좀 먹을래요? (mwo jom meogeullaeyo?) - What do you want to eat?

- 실례합니다. (sillyehamnida.) - Excuse me.

- 화장실 어디 있어요? (hwajangsil eodi isseoyo?) - Where is the bathroom?

- 내일 뭐 할 거예요? (naeil mwo hal geoyeyo?) - What are you doing tomorrow?

- 좀 더 느리게 말해주세요. (jom deo neurige malhaejuseyo.) - Can you speak more slowly?

- 잘 모르겠어요. (jal moreugesseoyo.) - I don't understand.

Other Tips:

- Remember to use the appropriate level of politeness when speaking to someone in Korean. This can depend on the situation, the age and social status of the person you're speaking to, and your own relationship with them.

- Use honorifics (such as -시 or -님) when speaking to someone who is older or of higher status than you.

- Practice your pronunciation! Korean is a language with its own unique sounds and intonations, so it can take some time to get used to speaking it fluently.

- Don't be afraid to make mistakes! The best way to learn a language is to practice speaking it as much as possible, even if you're not perfect at first.

Chapter 4: Numbers and Counting

In Korean, numbers and counting are an essential part of the language. Here are some basic numbers and counting expressions to get you started:

Numbers:

0: 영 (yeong)
1: 일 (il)
2: 이 (i)
3: 삼 (sam)
4: 사 (sa)
5: 오 (o)
6: 육 (yuk)
7: 칠 (chil)
8: 팔 (pal)
9: 구 (gu)
10: 십 (sip)

Counting expressions:

하나 (hana): one
둘 (dul): two
셋 (set): three
넷 (net): four
다섯 (daseot): five
여섯 (yeoseot): six
일곱 (ilgop): seven

여덟 (yeodeolb): eight
아홉 (ahop): nine
열 (yeol): ten

To count beyond ten, you can simply add the number to 십 (sip) to create multiples of ten. For example, 20 is 이십 (isip), 30 is 삼십 (samsip), and so on. To count in the hundreds, add the number to 백 (baek) and for thousands, add it to 천 (cheon). For example, 100 is 백 (baek), 200 is 이백 (ibaek), 1,000 is 천 (cheon), and 2,000 is 이천 (icheon).

You can also use the native Korean numbering system, which is used for counting objects, people, and hours. The first ten native Korean numbers are as follows:

하나 (hana): one
둘 (dul): two
셋 (set): three
넷 (net): four
다섯 (daseot): five
여섯 (yeoseot): six
일곱 (ilgop): seven
여덟 (yeodeolb): eight
아홉 (ahop): nine
열 (yeol): ten

To count beyond ten, simply add the native Korean numbers to the base number. For example, 11 is 열하나 (yeolhana), 12 is 열둘 (yeoldul), and so on.

To count in the native Korean system, you can use the following words:

- 개 (gae): for counting general objects

- 명 (myeong): for counting people
- 시 (si): for counting hours

For example, to say "two books," you would say "책 둘 (chaek dul) 개 (gae)." To say "four people," you would say "사람 넷 (saram net) 명 (myeong)." And to say "3 o'clock," you would say "세 시 (se si)."

In addition to these basic expressions, there are some special number-related expressions that you might find useful in everyday life. For example:

- 몇 (myeot): "how many" or "what number." This word can be used to ask for a specific number, such as "몇 시 (myeot si)?" ("What time is it?")
- 모두 (modu): "all" or "altogether." This word can be used to express a total number, such as "모두 다섯 (modu daseot)" ("Five in total").
- 반 (ban): "half." This word is used to express half of a number, such as "한 병 (han byeong) 반 (ban)" ("half a bottle").

When counting objects, the counter word 개 (gae) is used for most objects. However, there are some exceptions where specific counter words are used, such as 장 (jang) for flat objects like papers, 갑 (gap) for hats, and 병 (byeong) for bottles.

In addition to the native Korean numbering system, there is also a sino-Korean numbering system that uses Chinese characters. This system is often used for larger numbers and for counting money. For example, 100,000 is 십만 (sipman) in native Korean numbering system, but in sino-Korean system it is 百萬 (baekman).

When counting money in Korean, the unit of currency is won (원). There are no cents in Korean currency, so you can simply use the number of won for the amount. For example, 1,000 won is 천 원 (cheon won) and 50,000 won is 오만 원 (oman won).

When telling time in Korean, the hour is expressed first, followed by 분 (bun) for minutes. For example, 3:30 is 세 시 (se si) 삼십 분 (samsip bun). It's worth noting that the Korean language uses a 12-hour clock system, so to distinguish between morning and afternoon, you can add 오전 (ojeon) for AM and 오후 (ohu) for PM.

Korean has a unique counting system for ages. Instead of counting the years since birth, Koreans consider everyone to be one year old at birth, and then add a year on New Year's Day (January 1st). This means that a person who was born in December is considered to be two years old on New Year's Day.

Chapter 5: Korean Grammar Basics

Korean grammar can be complex, but here are some basics:

Sentence Structure: Korean sentences typically follow a subject-object-verb (SOV) structure, which means that the subject comes first, followed by the object, and then the verb. For example: "I eat rice" would be "나는 밥을 먹어요" (na-neun bap-eul meo-geo-yo).

Particles: Particles are used to indicate the grammatical relationships between words in a sentence. For example, the particle "을/를" (eul/reul) is used to indicate the direct object of a sentence. In the sentence "I eat rice," "rice" would be the direct object, and so it would be followed by "을/를": "나는 밥을 먹어요" (na-neun bap-eul meo-geo-yo).

Verb Endings: Korean verbs have different endings depending on tense and formality. For example, the present tense polite form of the verb "to eat" is "먹어요" (meo-geo-yo), while the past tense polite form is "먹었어요" (meo-geosseo-yo). The verb ending changes depending on the tense, formality, and whether the subject is singular or plural.

Honorifics: Korean has a complex system of honorifics that are used to show respect to others. This includes using different verb endings and titles depending on the social status of the person you are speaking to. For example, when speaking to someone older or of higher status, you would use the honorific title "오빠" (oppa) for an older brother or male friend, or "아저씨" (ajeossi) for an older man.

Adjectives: Adjectives in Korean come before the noun they modify. For example, "big house" would be "큰 집" (keun jip). Adjectives can also be used as predicates, meaning they can be used to describe the subject of a sentence. For example, "I am happy" would be "저는 행복해요" (jeo-neun haeng-bok-hae-yo).

Negation: To make a negative sentence in Korean, you can add the word "안" (an) before the verb. For example, "I don't eat rice" would be "나는 밥을 안 먹어요" (na-neun bap-eul an meo-geo-yo).

Verb Conjugation: Korean verbs can be conjugated based on a variety of factors, such as tense, formality, and politeness level. There are several verb endings for each tense, which can be used depending on the situation. For example, the past tense can be expressed using the -았/었 ending or the -었/였 ending, depending on the verb stem.

Politeness Levels: In addition to formal and informal language, Korean has several levels of politeness that can be used in different situations. The polite form (often called "jondaetmal") is the standard form used in most everyday situations, while the honorific form (often called "jondae-hamyeon mal") is used to show respect to people of higher status.

Sentence Ending Particles: In addition to the grammatical particles used throughout a sentence, Korean has specific particles that are used at the end of sentences to indicate various meanings. For example, the particle -요 is often used to indicate politeness or a request, while -네요 is used to express surprise or confirmation.

Sentence Connectives: Korean has a variety of connective words and phrases that are used to link sentences together. These include conjunctions like "그리고" (geurigo, "and") and "하지만" (hajiman, "but"), as well as adverbial connectives like "그래서" (geuraeseo, "so") and "그런데" (geureonde, "however").

Verb Stems: Korean verbs can be divided into two parts: the stem and the ending. The stem is the part of the verb that remains constant, while the ending changes depending on the tense and other factors. Some verb stems are irregular and may not follow the same pattern as regular verbs.

Pronouns: Korean pronouns can be tricky because they are often omitted in sentences when the subject is already clear from the context. However, some common pronouns include "나" (na, "I"), "너" (neo, "you"), and "우리" (uri, "we").

Topic/Comment Structure: In addition to the subject/object/verb structure, Korean also has a topic/comment structure. The topic is the part of the sentence that the speaker wants to bring attention to, while the comment is the information being conveyed about the topic. For example, in the sentence "이 책은 좋아요" (i chaek-eun joh-ayo), "이 책" (i chaek) is the topic and "좋아요" (joh-ayo) is the comment.

Honorific Speech: As mentioned earlier, Korean has a complex system of honorifics used to show respect to others. Honorific speech (jondaemal) involves using specific verb endings and sentence structures to show respect. For example, instead of saying "먹어" (meogeo) for "eat," you might use "드시다" (deusida) in honorific speech.

Counter Words: Korean has specific words used to count various objects. For example, when counting people, you would use the counter word "명" (myeong). So if you wanted to say "two people," you would say "두 명" (du myeong). There are different counter words for different types of objects.

Adverbs: Adverbs in Korean are used to describe the verb, adjective, or another adverb in a sentence. They often end in -게 (-ge) or -이 (-i). For example, the adverb "잘" (jal) means "well" and can be used to modify a verb like "먹다" (meokda, "eat") to become "잘 먹다" (jal meokda, "eat well").

Conditional Sentences: Korean has several ways to express conditional sentences. The most common way is to use "-으면" (-eumyeon) at the end of a sentence to indicate "if." For example, "If it rains, I will stay home" would be "비가 오면 집에 있을 거예요" (biga omyeon jibe isseul geoyeyo).

Imperative Form: The imperative form in Korean is used to give commands or make requests. It is formed by adding the ending "-아/어" (-a/eo) to the verb stem. For example, "Let's go!" would be "가자!" (gaja!), which is the imperative form of the verb "가다" (gada, "go").

Chapter 6: Adjectives and Adverbs

Korean adjectives are descriptive words that modify nouns and pronouns, while Korean adverbs modify verbs, adjectives, and other adverbs. Here are some commonly used Korean adjectives and adverbs:

Korean Adjectives:

- 좋다 (johta) - good
- 나쁘다 (nappeuda) - bad
- 예쁘다 (yeppeuda) - pretty
- 추운 (chuun) - cold
- 더운 (deoun) - hot
- 작다 (jakda) - small
- 크다 (keuda) - big
- 높다 (nopda) - high
- 낮다 (natda) - low
- 바쁘다 (bappeuda) – busy

Korean Adverbs:

- 잘 (jal) - well
- 빨리 (ppalli) - quickly
- 천천히 (cheoncheonhi) - slowly
- 자주 (jaju) - often
- 가끔 (gakkeum) - sometimes
- 거의 (geo-ui) - almost
- 너무 (neomu) - too much

- 아주 (aju) - very
- 조금 (jogeum) - a little
- 정말 (jeongmal) – really

Adjectives and adverbs are often used together in Korean sentences to provide a more detailed description of a noun or verb. For example, you might say "이 영화는 정말 재미있어요." (i yeonghwaneun jeongmal jaemiisseoyo) which means "this movie is really fun" where 정말 (jeongmal) is an adverb modifying the adjective 재미있어요 (jaemiisseoyo).

Adjectives and adverbs in Korean can change form depending on the tense, politeness level, and grammatical structure of the sentence. For example, the adjective 좋다 (johta) can be conjugated as 좋아요 (joayo) in polite form or 좋겠다 (johgetda) in future tense form.

Some adjectives and adverbs in Korean are actually derived from verbs, and their meanings can change depending on the context of the sentence. For example, the verb 늦다 (neutta) means "to be late," but the adverb 늦게 (neutge) means "late" as in "doing something late."

In some cases, adjectives and adverbs can be used interchangeably in Korean. For example, the adjective 빠른 (ppareun) means "fast," but you can also use the adverb 빨리 (ppalli) to convey the same meaning in some contexts.

Some adjectives and adverbs in Korean can have multiple meanings depending on the context of the sentence. For example, the adverb 또 (tto) can mean "again" or "also," depending on the situation.

Adjectives in Korean can be categorized into two main groups: descriptive adjectives and stative adjectives. Descriptive adjectives describe qualities that can change, such as size, color, or shape. Stative adjectives describe qualities that are relatively constant, such as emotions or physical states. For example, the adjective 예쁘다

(yeppeuda), meaning "pretty," is a descriptive adjective, while the adjective 행복하다 (haengbokhada), meaning "happy," is a stative adjective.

Adverbs in Korean can be categorized into several different types, including time adverbs, frequency adverbs, manner adverbs, and degree adverbs. Time adverbs indicate when an action takes place, frequency adverbs indicate how often an action occurs, manner adverbs describe how an action is performed, and degree adverbs indicate the degree or intensity of an action.

Korean adjectives and adverbs can be used to create comparative and superlative forms. For example, to create the comparative form of an adjective or adverb, you can add -으(ㅂ)ㄴ to the stem of the word. For example, the comparative form of the adjective 높다 (nopda), meaning "high," is 더 높다 (deo nopda), meaning "higher." To create the superlative form, you can add -est at the end of the word, or use the word 가장 (gajang), meaning "most." For example, the superlative form of the adjective 크다 (keuda), meaning "big," is 제일 크다 (jeil keuda), meaning "the biggest."

In some cases, Korean adjectives can be used as verbs by adding the verb ending -하다 (-hada) to the stem of the adjective. For example, the adjective 깨끗하다 (kkaekkeuthada), meaning "clean," can be used as a verb to mean "to clean."

Some Korean adverbs are formed by adding the suffix -이 (i) to a noun or adjective stem. For example, the noun 맛 (mat), meaning "taste," can be used to create the adverb 맛있게 (matitge), meaning "deliciously."

In Korean, some adjectives and adverbs can have both a positive and negative form. For example, the adjective 높다 (nopda), meaning "high," has a negative form 낮다 (natda), meaning "low." Similarly, the adverb 느리다 (neurida), meaning "slow," has a negative form 빠르다 (ppareuda), meaning "fast."

Some adjectives and adverbs in Korean can be used to express hypothetical or conditional situations. For example, the adverb 아마 (ama), meaning "maybe," can be used to express uncertainty, and the adverb 어쩌면 (eojjeomyeon), meaning "perhaps" or "possibly," can be used to express hypothetical situations.

Some Korean adjectives and adverbs can have different meanings depending on the context of the sentence. For example, the adverb 다시 (dasi) can mean "again" or "anew," depending on the situation.

In addition to their basic meanings, some Korean adjectives and adverbs can also have idiomatic or slang meanings. For example, the adverb 약간 (yakgan), meaning "a little," can be used to express sarcasm or irony in some contexts.

Adjectives and adverbs can be used to modify nouns, verbs, and other adjectives and adverbs in Korean. For example, the adverb 빠르게 (ppareuge), meaning "quickly," can modify the verb 달리다 (dallida), meaning "to run," to form the phrase 빠르게 달리다 (ppareuge dallida), meaning "to run quickly."

Chapter 7: Verbs and Tenses

In Korean, verbs are conjugated to reflect tense, mood, and politeness. The most basic form of a verb is its dictionary form or "root" form, which ends in "-다" (da) or "-하다" (hada). Here are some common tenses and verb endings in Korean:

Present tense: The present tense is the base form of the verb. For example, "to eat" is "먹다" (meokda) in Korean.

Past tense: To conjugate a verb in the past tense, add the suffix "-았/었-" (at/eot) to the root form. For example, "ate" in the past tense is "먹었다" (meogeotda).

Future tense: To express the future tense in Korean, you can use the auxiliary verb "-겠-" (get). For example, "I will eat" is "먹겠다" (meokgetda).

Present continuous tense: The present continuous tense in Korean is formed by adding the suffix "-고 있다" (go itda) to the root form of the verb. For example, "I am eating" is "먹고 있다" (meokgo itda).

Past continuous tense: The past continuous tense is formed by adding the suffix "-고 있었다" (go isseotda) to the root form. For example, "I was eating" is "먹고 있었다" (meokgo isseotda).

Conditional mood: The conditional mood in Korean is expressed by using the suffix "-으면" (eumyeon) after the root form of the verb. For example, "If I eat" is "먹으면" (meogeumyeon).

Imperative mood: To give commands or make requests in Korean, use the imperative mood. To form the imperative, add the suffix "-아/어" (a/eo) to the root form of the verb. For example, "Eat!" is "먹어!" (meogeo!).

Politeness levels: In Korean, the level of politeness can be reflected in the verb conjugation. There are different endings for verbs depending on the level of formality required in a given situation. For example, "-요" (yo) is often added to verbs to make them more polite. The three main levels are formal, informal, and intimate. Formal language is used when speaking to someone of higher status or in formal situations, while informal and intimate language are used among friends and family.

Honorifics: In addition to politeness levels, Korean also has an honorific system for showing respect to people of higher status. Honorific verbs are used when speaking to or about someone who is older or more respected. These verbs have different endings than regular verbs.

Aspect: In addition to tense, Korean verbs also convey aspect, which refers to the way an action is viewed in relation to time. There are two aspects in Korean: the perfective aspect, which indicates that an action has been completed, and the imperfective aspect, which indicates that an action is ongoing or incomplete.

Auxiliary verbs: Korean has a number of auxiliary verbs that are used to convey various meanings, such as obligation, possibility, and permission. These verbs are often combined with the base form of a main verb to create a new meaning. For example, the auxiliary verb "-겠-" (get) can be added to the end of a verb to express future tense or probability. "할 거예요" (hal geoyeyo) means "I will do" but "할 거겠어요" (hal geosseoyo) means "I think I will do."

Verb endings: In addition to the endings mentioned above, there are many other verb endings in Korean that convey different meanings, such as "-자" (ja), which means "let's," or "-네요" (neyo), which is used to express surprise or curiosity.

Word order: In Korean, the verb usually comes at the end of the sentence, after the subject and object. This means that the verb ending can be a crucial indicator of tense, mood, and politeness.

Subject and object markers: In Korean, the subject and object of a sentence are marked with particles, which come after the noun. The subject particle is "-이/가" (i/ga) and the object particle is "-을/를" (eul/reul). These particles help to clarify the sentence structure and make it easier to understand who is doing what.

Passive voice: In Korean, the passive voice is formed by using the auxiliary verb "-이/히" (i/hi) after the root form of the verb. For example, "I was hit" is "맞혔다" (majhyeotda). Note that some verbs may change their vowel sound when used in the passive voice.

Causative verbs: Korean has causative verbs, which are used to express the idea of causing someone to do something. To form the causative, add the suffix "-게 하다" (ge hada) after the root form of the verb. For example, "make me eat" is "먹게 해라" (meokge haera).

Negation: To form the negative form of a verb in Korean, add the suffix "-지 않다" (ji anhda) after the root form. For example, "I don't eat" is "먹지 않다" (meokji anhda).

Conjunctions: In Korean, conjunctions are often used to connect two clauses or sentences together. Common conjunctions include "그리고" (geurigo) for "and," "그러나" (geureona) for "but," and "그래서" (geuraeseo) for "therefore."

Honorific verbs: As I mentioned earlier, Korean has an honorific system for showing respect to people of higher status. Honorific verbs are formed by adding the suffix "-시-" (si) after the root form of the verb. For example, "eat" is "드시다" (deusida) in the honorific form.

Conditional tense: In Korean, the conditional tense is used to express hypothetical situations or conditions. To form the conditional tense, add the suffix "-면" (myeon) after the root form of the verb. For example, "if it rains" is "비가 오면" (biga omyeon).

Future tense: Unlike many other languages, Korean doesn't have a separate future tense. Instead, the present tense is often used to indicate future actions or events. For example, "I will eat" is "먹을 거예요" (meogeul geoyeyo), which literally means "I am going to eat."

Conjunctive endings: In Korean, there are several conjunctive endings that can be used to join clauses together. Some examples include "-고" (go) for "and," "-서" (seo) for "so," and "-으니까" (eunikka) for "because."

Honorific endings: In addition to honorific verbs, Korean also has honorific endings that can be added to regular verbs to show respect for the listener or subject of the sentence. These endings include "-시-" (si) and "-으시-" (eusi).

Tense markers: In Korean, tense markers are often used to indicate past or present tense. Some examples of tense markers include "-았/었-" (at/eot) for past tense and "-고 있다" (go itda) for present continuous tense.

Reflexive verbs: Korean has reflexive verbs, which are used to indicate that the subject of the sentence is also the object of the action. To form a reflexive verb, add the suffix "-(으)ㄹ" ((eu)l) after the root form of the verb. For example, "I wash myself" is "나는 내가 씻을 거예요" (naneun naega ssiseul geoyeyo).

Irregular verbs: Like many languages, Korean has some irregular verbs that don't follow the typical rules of conjugation. Some common irregular verbs include "하다" (hada) for "to do," "오다" (oda) for "to come," and "가다" (gada) for "to go."

Adjectives as verbs: In Korean, some adjectives can be used as verbs. For example, the adjective "좋다" (jota) means "good," but it can also be used as a verb meaning "to like." "나는 과자를 좋아해요" (naneun gwajareul johahae yo) means "I like cookies."

Reported speech: In Korean, reported speech (also known as indirect speech) is formed using the verb "하다" (hada) after the quoted speech. For example, "He said he was tired" is "그는 지쳤다고 했다" (geuneun jichyeotdago haetda).

Chapter 8: Nouns and Articles

Korean nouns are words that represent people, objects, places, ideas, and concepts. Unlike many other languages, Korean nouns do not have gender. However, they do have number, which means that they can be singular or plural.

Korean does not have articles like "a" or "the" in English. Instead, the specificity of a noun is often determined by context and the use of particles. The particle "은/는" (eun/neun) is used to mark the topic of a sentence, while the particle "이/가" (i/ga) is used to mark the subject. When a noun is marked with these particles, it becomes more specific and identifiable in the context of the sentence.

There are also demonstrative pronouns in Korean that can be used to indicate whether a noun is specific or general. The word "이" (i) is used to indicate a specific noun that is close to the speaker, while the word "그" (geu) is used to indicate a specific noun that is close to the listener. The word "저" (jeo) is used to indicate a noun that is far from both the speaker and the listener.

In addition, there are also possessive particles that can be used to show ownership or possession of a noun. The particle "의" (ui) is used to indicate possession, for example, "나의 책" (naui chaek) meaning "my book."

Number: Korean nouns can be either singular or plural. To make a noun plural, the particle "들" (deul) is often added after the noun. For example, "사과" (sagwa) means "apple," while "사과들" (sagwadeul) means "apples."

Classifier particles: In Korean, classifier particles are used to indicate the quantity or measure of a noun. For example, the particle "개" (gae) is used to count animals, while the particle "잔" (jan) is used to count glasses of liquid.

Counting system: Korean has two counting systems, the native Korean system and the Sino-Korean system. The native Korean system is used for counting small objects and things, while the Sino-Korean system is used for counting larger quantities and time.

Honorifics: Korean also has a complex system of honorifics, which are used to show respect and politeness to the person being referred to. Different forms of nouns and particles are used depending on the level of politeness and respect required.

Compound nouns: Korean often uses compound nouns, which are formed by combining two or more words. For example, "학생" (haksaeng) means "student," and is formed by combining "학교" (hakgyo) meaning "school," and "생" (saeng) meaning "person."

Articles in loanwords: Some Korean loanwords from English or other languages may include articles like "a" or "the" in their Korean spelling, but these are not part of the Korean grammar system and are only included to match the original language.

Topic and subject markers: In addition to the particles "은/는" (eun/neun) and "이/가" (i/ga) that mark the topic and subject of a sentence, Korean also has other particles that are used to mark other sentence elements. For example, the particle "을/를" (eul/reul) is used to mark the direct object of a sentence.

Adjective endings: Korean adjectives are used to describe or modify nouns, and they have different endings depending on the level of formality and politeness required. For example, the adjective "좋다"

(jota) means "good," but when used in a polite context, it becomes "좋습니다" (jotseumnida).

Noun phrases: In Korean, noun phrases can be formed by combining a noun with other words or phrases, including adjectives, verbs, and other nouns. For example, the phrase "큰 집" (keun jip) means "big house," and is formed by combining the adjective "큰" (keun) meaning "big," with the noun "집" (jip) meaning "house."

Compound particles: In addition to particles that mark sentence elements, Korean also has compound particles that are used to indicate more complex relationships between words in a sentence. For example, the particle "으로" (euro) is used to indicate the means by which something is done or achieved, while the particle "에서" (eseo) is used to indicate the location where something happens.

Pronouns: Korean has several types of pronouns, including personal pronouns, demonstrative pronouns, and interrogative pronouns. Personal pronouns can vary depending on the level of politeness required, while demonstrative pronouns and interrogative pronouns have different forms depending on whether they are used as subjects or objects.

Proper nouns: Proper nouns in Korean are written with the first letter capitalized, and include names of people, places, organizations, and more. For example, "김철수" (Kim Cheol-su) is a common Korean name, while "한강" (Han River) is the name of a river that runs through Seoul.

Declension: Korean nouns do not decline based on grammatical case like some other languages do, such as Latin or Russian. Instead, particles are added to the end of the noun to indicate its function in the sentence.

Measure words: Like classifier particles, Korean also has measure words that are used to indicate the amount or quantity of something.

For example, "한 병" (han byeong) means "one bottle," and the measure word "병" (byeong) is used to indicate that it is a container of liquid.

Chapter 9: Questions and Negation

In Korean, questions can be formed in a few different ways depending on the situation and the level of formality. Negation is also important in forming negative sentences. Here are some common ways to form questions and negations in Korean:

Adding the particle "이/가" at the end of a sentence: This is a simple way to form a question in Korean. Simply add the particle "이/가" at the end of a sentence to turn it into a question. For example, "뭐 해?" (What are you doing?) or "오늘 날씨가 좋아요?" (Is the weather nice today?)

Using the question word "어떻게" (how) or "무엇" (what): These words can be used to form more specific questions. For example, "어떻게 가요?" (How do I get there?) or "무엇을 먹을까요?" (What should we eat?)

Using the verb ending "-니" or "-냐": This is a more formal way to form a question in Korean. For example, "먹었니?" (Did you eat?) or "왔냐?" (Did you come?)

Using the verb ending "-지 않다": This is the negative form of a verb in Korean. For example, "먹지 않다" (not eat) or "가지 않다" (not go).

Using the negative adverb "안": This is another way to form a negative sentence in Korean. For example, "안 먹어요" (I don't eat) or "안 가요" (I'm not going).

It's important to note that the level of formality and politeness in Korean is very important, so the above examples may differ depending on the context and the person you are speaking with. When speaking with someone who is older or of higher social status, it's important to use more polite language. In these situations, it's common to use honorific verbs and endings, such as "-시" instead of "-요" and "-습니다" instead of "-요".

Question words: In addition to "어떻게" and "무엇", there are other question words in Korean, such as "언제" (when), "어디" (where), "누구" (who), and "왜" (why).

Inverted word order: In Korean, the word order in a question is often inverted compared to a statement. For example, "당신은 한국 사람이에요" (You are Korean) would become "한국 사람이에요, 당신은?" (You are Korean, right?)

Negative questions: In Korean, negative questions can be formed by using the negative verb ending "-지 않다" or the negative adverb "안" along with a question word. For example, "어디에 안 가?" (Where are you not going?) or "뭐 안 먹어?" (What aren't you eating?)

Formal negation: In formal situations, it's common to use the negative form of a verb instead of "안". For example, "들어가지 않습니다" (I'm not going in) instead of "안 들어가요".

Rising intonation: In Korean, questions are often accompanied by a rising intonation at the end of the sentence. This can help to indicate that the speaker is asking a question, even if the word order or particles are the same as in a statement.

Tag questions: In Korean, tag questions can be formed by adding the particle "지 않아" or "잖아" at the end of a sentence. For example,

"비가 오지 않아?" (It's not raining, right?) or "이것은 맛있잖아?" (This is delicious, isn't it?)

Double negation: In some cases, Korean uses a double negation to emphasize a negative statement. This is done by using both the negative verb ending "-지 않다" and the negative adverb "안". For example, "나는 결코 먹지 않습니다" (I definitely won't eat).

Alternative question: In Korean, an alternative question can be formed by using the conjunction "아니면" (or). For example, "우유 아니면 주스?" (Milk or juice?)

Complex sentences: Korean allows for complex sentences with multiple clauses, making it possible to form questions and negations with more detailed information. For example, "저는 내일 친구를 만날 거예요. 그러니까 오늘 밤에는 일찍 자려고 해요." (I'm meeting a friend tomorrow, so I'm planning to go to bed early tonight.)

Intonation patterns: In Korean, there are different intonation patterns for yes-no questions and information questions. Yes-no questions often have a rising-falling intonation, while information questions have a rising intonation throughout the sentence.

Wh-questions: In Korean, wh-questions can be formed by using question words such as "누구" (who), "어디" (where), "언제" (when), "왜" (why), "어떻게" (how), and "무엇" (what). For example, "누구세요?" (Who are you?), "어디에서 왔어요?" (Where are you from?), or "왜 그렇게 생각하세요?" (Why do you think that way?)

Negative imperative: In Korean, the negative imperative can be formed by adding the negative verb ending "-지 마세요" to the stem of a verb. For example, "먹지 마세요" (Don't eat), or "가지 마세요" (Don't go).

Negative adjectives: In Korean, adjectives can also be negated by adding the negative verb ending "-지 않다". For example, "바쁘지 않아요." (I'm not busy), or "작지 않아요." (It's not small).

Passive voice: In Korean, the passive voice can be used to describe actions done to the subject of a sentence. For example, "나는 친구에게 선물을 받았어요." (I received a gift from my friend) can be changed to "나는 친구에게서 선물을 받았어요." (I received a gift from my friend, with the subject being emphasized).

Honorific language: In formal situations, it's important to use honorific language to show respect to the listener. This can involve using honorific verbs and endings, as well as avoiding the use of first-person pronouns.

Chapter 10: Korean Honorifics

Korean honorifics are an important aspect of Korean language and culture. They are used to show respect and politeness to others, especially to those who are older or in a higher social position. Here are some of the most common Korean honorifics:

존댓말 (jondaetmal) - This is the formal and polite form of speech used when speaking to someone who is older or in a higher position. It involves using honorific verb endings, such as -시- (-shi-) or -으시- (-eushi-), and honorific nouns, such as 선생님 (seonsaengnim) for teacher or 사장님 (sajangnim) for CEO.

반말 (banmal) - This is the informal and casual form of speech used when speaking to someone who is younger or in a lower position. It involves dropping the honorific verb endings and using regular verb endings instead, such as -어/-아 (-eo/-a) or -어요/-아요 (-eoyo/-ayo).

호칭 (hoching) - This is the title or address used when referring to someone. There are different titles and addresses depending on the person's age and social position. For example, older brothers are called 형 (hyeong) and older sisters are called 누나 (nuna) by younger siblings.

존댓말 + 호칭 (jondaetmal + hoching) - This is a combination of formal language and titles used when speaking to someone who is older or in a higher position. For example, someone might use 선생님 (seonsaengnim) with 존댓말 (jondaetmal) to address their teacher.

연하게 (yeonhage) - This is a polite and respectful way of speaking that is used between people who are close in age or social position. It is less formal than 존댓말 (jondaetmal) but more polite than 반말 (banmal).

존경어 (jongyeongeo) - This is a very formal and polite form of speech used to show deep respect and admiration. It is often used in official or ceremonial settings, such as when addressing a king or queen.

Honorific suffixes: In addition to the honorific verb endings and nouns mentioned earlier, there are also honorific suffixes that can be added to someone's name or title to show respect. For example, -님 (-nim) is a common honorific suffix used with job titles or names to show respect. For example, a doctor might be called 의사님 (uisanim) instead of just 의사 (uisa) when using polite language.

Context is important: Korean honorifics can be complex and vary depending on the situation, so it's important to pay attention to context and adjust your language accordingly. For example, you might use more formal language and titles when meeting someone for the first time or in a professional setting.

Different levels of formality: There are different levels of formality within the formal language (존댓말, jondaetmal) and informal language (반말, banmal) categories. For example, there are different levels of politeness within 존댓말 (jondaetmal) depending on how much respect you want to show.

Honorifics in writing: Korean honorifics are also used in writing, such as in emails, letters, and other formal documents. In written communication, it's especially important to use the appropriate honorific language and titles based on the recipient's social position and relationship to you.

Honorifics and age: Age is an important factor in Korean honorifics, as respect is often shown to those who are older. This is reflected in the titles and suffixes used to address older people, such as 아버님 (abeonim) for father and 할머니 (halmeoni) for grandmother.

Honorifics in conversation: In addition to using honorific language and titles when addressing someone directly, Korean honorifics also play a role in conversations. For example, if someone mentions a person of higher status or age, they might use honorific language to refer to that person, even if they are not directly addressing them.

Honorifics and gender: While Korean honorifics are generally used based on age and social status, there are also some gender-specific honorifics. For example, the honorific suffix -씨 (-ssi) can be used for both men and women, but there is also a female-specific suffix -양 (-yang) that can be used to show respect for women.

Honorifics and family relationships: Korean honorifics also play a role in family relationships. For example, children will often use honorific language and titles when speaking to their parents or grandparents, even though they are family members. This shows respect for their elders and reflects the importance of age and hierarchy in Korean culture.

Honorifics and business culture: Korean honorifics are especially important in business settings, where showing respect and building relationships are key. It's common to use formal language and titles when speaking to colleagues or business partners, and to show extra respect to those in higher positions.

Honorifics and language learning: Learning Korean honorifics can be challenging for non-native speakers, but it's an important aspect of language learning. In addition to understanding the grammar rules and vocabulary, learners also need to be able to use honorific language and titles appropriately to show respect and build relationships with Korean speakers.

Honorifics and social status: In addition to age and gender, social status also plays a role in Korean honorifics. For example, someone who holds a high-ranking position, such as a government official or CEO, might be addressed with even more formal language and titles to show respect for their status.

Honorifics and body language: In addition to language, body language can also be used to show respect in Korean culture. For example, bowing is a common way to show respect, and the depth and length of the bow can vary depending on the level of respect being shown.

Honorifics in media: Korean honorifics are also present in media such as TV shows, movies, and music. For example, characters might use honorific language when speaking to their elders or people of higher status, and honorific titles might be used to refer to characters in formal situations.

Honorifics in everyday life: Korean honorifics are not just reserved for formal situations, but are also used in everyday life. For example, a younger person might use honorific language when speaking to an older person, even if they are just friends. This reflects the importance of showing respect for elders and building positive relationships in Korean culture.

Honorifics and language change: Like all languages, Korean is constantly evolving, and the use of honorifics is no exception. In recent years, there has been a trend towards using more informal language and titles, particularly among younger generations. However, it's still important to be aware of and use appropriate honorifics in formal situations.

Chapter 11: Korean Vocabulary

Family vocabulary:

가족 (gajok) - family
부모님 (bumonim) - parents
아버지 (abeoji) - father
어머니 (eomeoni) - mother
아들 (adeul) - son
딸 (ttal) - daughter
형 (hyeong) - older brother
오빠 (oppa) - older brother (used by younger sisters)
누나 (nuna) - older sister (used by younger siblings)
여동생 (yeodongsaeng) - younger sister
남동생 (namdongsaeng) - younger brother
할아버지 (harabeoji) - grandfather
할머니 (halmuhni) - grandmother
손자 (sonja) - grandson
손녀 (sonnyeo) - granddaughter
삼촌 (samchon) - uncle (father's younger brother)
아저씨 (ajeossi) - uncle (father's friend or a stranger)
이모 (imo) - aunt (father's younger sister)
아줌마 (ajumma) - aunt (mother's friend or a stranger)
숙모 (sukmo) - aunt (mother's younger sister)
시아버지 (siabeoji) - great-grandfather
시어머니 (siumeoni) - great-grandmother
사촌 (sachon) - cousin

조부모님 (jobumonim) - grandparents (paternal)
외할머니 (oehalmuhni) - grandmother (father's mother-in-law)
이모부 (imobu) - uncle (mother's brother-in-law)
시아버님 (siabeonim) - great-uncle
시어머님 (siumeonim) - great-aunt
며느리 (myeoneuri) - daughter-in-law
사위 (sawi) - son-in-law
시누이 (sinui) - daughter-in-law (married to oldest son)
장인어른 (jangineoreun) - father-in-law
장모님 (jangmonim) - mother-in-law

Time vocabulary:

시간 (sigan) - time
분 (bun) - minute
초 (cho) - second
시 (si) - hour
오전 (ojeon) - morning
오후 (ohu) - afternoon
저녁 (jeonyeok) - evening
밤 (bam) - night
오늘 (oneul) - today
내일 (naeil) - tomorrow
어제 (eoje) - yesterday
주 (ju) - week
월 (wol) - month
연도 (yeondo) - year
시계 (sigye) - clock/watch
알람 (allam) - alarm
일찍 (iljjik) - early
늦게 (neutge) - late
지금 (jigeum) - now
언제 (eonje) - when
몇 시 (myeot si) - what time
오래 (orae) - long time
짧게 (jjalbge) - short time
매일 (maeil) - every day
매주 (maeju) - every week
매달 (maedal) - every month
매년 (maenyeon) - every year
새벽 (saebyeok) - dawn, early morning

Colors vocabulary:

빨강 (ppalgang) - red
주황 (juhwang) - orange
노랑 (norang) - yellow
초록 (chorok) - green
파랑 (parang) - blue
남색 (namsaek) - navy blue
보라 (bora) - purple
핑크 (pingkeu) - pink
갈색 (galsaek) - brown
회색 (hoesaek) - gray
검정 (geomjeong) - black
흰색 (hwaensaek) - white
진한 (jinhan) - dark
연한 (yeonhan) - light

Weather vocabulary:

날씨 (nalssi) - weather
맑은 (malgeun) - clear
흐린 (heurin) - cloudy
비 (bi) - rain
눈 (nun) - snow
구름 (gureum) - cloud
태풍 (taepung) - typhoon
폭풍 (pokpung) - storm
번개 (beongae) - lightning
천둥 (cheondung) - thunder
바람 (baram) - wind
열대야 (yeoldaeya) - heatwave
한파 (hanpa) - cold wave
추운 (chuun) - cold
더운 (deoun) - hot
습한 (seuphan) - humid
건조한 (geonjohan) - dry
해발 (haebal) - altitude
기압 (giap) - air pressure
온도 (ondo) - temperature
안개 (angae) - fog
우박 (ubak) - hail
화창한 (hwachanghan) - sunny
얼음 (eoreum) - ice

Animals vocabulary:

동물 (dongmul) - animal
개 (gae) - dog
고양이 (goyangi) - cat
새 (sae) - bird
쥐 (jwi) - mouse
곰 (gom) - bear
호랑이 (horangi) - tiger
사자 (saja) - lion
원숭이 (wonsung-i) - monkey
코끼리 (kokkiri) - elephant
기린 (girin) - giraffe
하마 (hama) - hippopotamus
물고기 (mulgogi) - fish
상어 (sang-eo) - shark
고래 (gore) - whale
뱀 (baem) - snake
거북이 (geobugi) - turtle
사다리꼴 (sadari-gol) - crocodile
개구리 (gaeguri) - frog
돼지 (dwaeji) - pig
소 (so) - cow
말 (mal) - horse
양 (yang) - sheep
닭 (dak) - chicken
오리 (ori) - duck
벌 (beol) - bee
나비 (nabi) - butterfly
여우 (yeo-u) - fox
늑대 (neukdae) - wolf
사슴 (saseum) - deer

Transportation vocabulary:

교통 (gyotong) - transportation, traffic
차 (cha) - car
버스 (beoseu) - bus
지하철 (jihacheol) - subway
택시 (taeksi) - taxi
자전거 (jajeongeo) - bicycle
비행기 (bihaenggi) - airplane
배 (bae) - boat, ship
기차 (gicha) - train
트럭 (teureok) - truck
오토바이 (oto-bai) - motorcycle
승용차 (seung-yong-cha) - sedan
전철 (jeoncheol) - light rail
고속도로 (gosokdoro) - highway
자동차 (jadong-cha) - automobile
지진 (jijin) - earthquake
출퇴근 (chultoegyeom) - commute
터미널 (teomineol) - terminal
주차장 (jucha-jang) - parking lot
공항 (gonghang) - airport
버스 정류장 (beoseu jeongnyujang) - bus stop
간선도로 (ganseon-doro) - arterial road
자가용 (jagayong) - private car

Food vocabulary:

음식 (eumsik) - food
밥 (bap) - cooked rice
김치 (kimchi) - fermented cabbage
불고기 (bulgogi) - marinated grilled beef
비빔밥 (bibimbap) - mixed rice with vegetables and beef
된장 (doenjang) - soybean paste
갈비 (galbi) - marinated grilled beef or pork ribs
냉면 (naengmyeon) - cold buckwheat noodles
만두 (mandu) - dumplings
떡볶이 (tteokbokki) - stir-fried rice cake
미역국 (miyeokguk) - seaweed soup
삼계탕 (samgyetang) - chicken ginseng soup
해물찜 (haemuljjim) - steamed seafood
김밥 (kimbap) - rice and vegetable rolled in seaweed
순두부찌개 (sundubujjigae) - soft tofu stew
오뎅 (odeng) - fish cake
치킨 (chikin) - fried chicken
피자 (piza) - pizza
햄버거 (haembeogeoe) - hamburger
스파게티 (seupaget-i) - spaghetti
샐러드 (saelleodeu) - salad
빵 (ppang) - bread
케이크 (keikeu) - cake
아이스크림 (aiseukeurim) - ice cream
커피 (keopi) - coffee
차 (cha) - tea
맥주 (maekju) - beer
소주 (soju) - Korean rice wine
막걸리 (makgeolli) - Korean rice wine (milky white)
밀크티 (milkuti) - milk tea

Clothing vocabulary:

옷 (ot) - clothing
바지 (baji) - pants
스커트 (seukeoteu) - skirt
원피스 (wonpiseu) - dress
셔츠 (syeocheu) - shirt
티셔츠 (tisyeocheu) - T-shirt
맨투맨 (maentuman) - sweatshirt
후드티 (hudeuti) - hoodie
슬리브리스 (seullibeuriseu) - sleeveless shirt
자켓 (jaket) - jacket
코트 (koteu) - coat
니트 (niteu) - knitwear
양말 (yangmal) - socks
구두 (gudu) - shoes
운동화 (undonghwa) - sneakers
샌들 (saendeul) - sandals
슬리퍼 (seullipeo) - slippers
모자 (moja) - hat
안경 (angyeong) - eyeglasses
팔찌 (pallji) - bracelet
목걸이 (mokgeori) - necklace
귀걸이 (gwigeori) - earrings
반지 (banji) - ring
시계 (sigye) - watch
지갑 (jigap) - wallet
벨트 (belteu) - belt
넥타이 (nekta-i) - necktie
스카프 (seukapeu) - scarf
머플러 (meopeulleo) - muffler
비니 (bini) - beanie

Emotions vocabulary:

기쁨 (gippeum) - joy, happiness
슬픔 (seulpeum) - sadness
화남 (hwanam) - anger
불안 (buran) - anxiety
신뢰 (sinlyu) - trust
좌절 (jwajeol) - frustration, disappointment
희망 (huimang) - hope
불만 (bulman) - dissatisfaction
불쾌함 (bulkwoeham) - discomfort
혼란 (honran) - confusion
설렘 (seolleum) - excitement
사랑 (sarang) - love
우울함 (uulham) - depression
신기함 (sinkiham) - amazement, surprise
미안 (mian) - sorry
감사 (gamsa) - gratitude
부끄러움 (bukkeureoum) - shyness, embarrassment
짜증 (jja jeung) - annoyance
만족 (manjok) - satisfaction
창피함 (changpiham) - shame, humiliation
의심 (uisim) - suspicion
놀람 (nollam) - astonishment, shock
즐거움 (jeulgeoum) - enjoyment, pleasure
경악 (gyeong-ak) - consternation, dismay
혐오 (hyeom-o) - disgust, hatred
열등감 (yeoldeung-gam) - inferiority complex
자부심 (jabusim) - pride, self-esteem

Chapter 12: Korean Idioms and Expressions

Korean idioms and expressions are commonly used phrases that convey a certain meaning or message that may not be readily apparent from the literal meaning of the words. These idioms and expressions often reflect Korean culture, history, and values.

Here are a few examples of common Korean idioms and expressions:

- "고래 싸움에 새우 등 터진다." (Gorae ssawoomae saeu deung teojinda) - "When whales fight, the shrimp's back is broken." This expression is used to describe a situation in which two powerful entities or individuals are in conflict, and weaker parties are often caught in the crossfire.

- "소 잃고 외양간 고친다." (So irgo oeyanggan gochinda) - "After losing the cow, one repairs the barn." This idiom refers to the idea that sometimes people neglect important things until it's too late, and only take action once something has been lost or damaged.

- "산 넘어 산." (San neomeo san) - "A mountain beyond a mountain." This expression is used to describe a seemingly endless series of challenges or difficulties that must be overcome.

- "백지장도 맞들면 낫다." (Baekjijangdo matdeulmyeon natda) - "Even a blank sheet of paper has its uses if you hold it together." This idiom is used to emphasize the importance of teamwork and cooperation, and the idea that even the smallest contribution can make a difference.

- "입이 가볍다." (Ibi gabyeopda) - "One's mouth is light." This expression is used to describe a person who is talkative or prone to gossip.

- "눈치가 빠르다." (Nunchiga ppareuda) - "One has quick 'nunchi'." Nunchi is a concept in Korean culture that refers to the ability to quickly perceive and respond to the mood and feelings of others. This expression is used to describe someone who is good at reading the room and adjusting their behavior accordingly.

- "한강의 물이 다른 강의 물을 못 막는다." (Hangangeui muri dareun gangui mureul mot makneunda) - "The water of the Han River cannot block the water of another river." This expression is used to describe the idea that no one can stop the inevitable or prevent a natural progression of events.

- "귀신도 모르는 밥상." (Gwisindo moreuneun babsang) - "A dinner table where even ghosts are not aware." This expression is used to describe a situation where there is an abundant and delicious feast that nobody wants to miss.

- "고양이한테 생선을 맡기다." (Goyangihante saengseoneul matgida) - "To entrust fish to a cat." This expression is used to describe a situation where you give responsibility to someone who is not trustworthy or unreliable.

- "천리 길도 한 걸음부터." (Cheonri gildo han georeumbuteo) - "A journey of a thousand miles begins with a single step." This idiom emphasizes the importance of taking action and starting small to achieve a larger goal.

- "남의 떡이 더 커보인다." (Namui tteogi deo keoboinda) - "Other people's rice cakes look bigger." This expression is used to describe the tendency to envy what others have and not appreciate one's own blessings.

- "똥 묻은 개가 겨 묻은 개 나무란다." (Ttong mudeun gaega gyeo mudeun gae namurannda) - "A dog with feces on its nose scolds a dog with hay on its nose." This expression is used to describe someone who is hypocritical and criticizes others for the same faults that they have.

- "우물 안 개구리." (Umul an gaeguri) - "A frog in a well." This expression is used to describe someone who is narrow-minded and has a limited perspective on the world.

- "산중턱도 말보다." (Sanjungteokdo malboda) - "The middle of a mountain is better than words." This expression is used to emphasize the importance of action over words, and the idea that experiencing something firsthand is more valuable than hearing about it from others.

Chapter 13: Korean Culture and Etiquette

Korean culture and etiquette are deeply rooted in Confucianism, which emphasizes respect for authority, hierarchy, and the importance of relationships. Here are some key aspects of Korean culture and etiquette:

Bowing: Bowing is an important gesture of respect in Korean culture. When greeting someone, it's customary to bow slightly. The depth and duration of the bow depend on the status and age of the person being greeted.

Handshakes: Handshakes are also common in Korea, especially in business settings. However, it's important to use a gentle grip and not to hold on for too long.

Removing shoes: It's customary to remove shoes before entering a Korean home or some traditional Korean buildings. Look for a shoe rack or a designated area to leave your shoes.

Addressing others: When addressing someone who is older or has a higher status, it's polite to use honorific titles, such as "ajumma" (for middle-aged women) or "sunbae" (for someone who has more experience in a particular field).

Gift-giving: Gift-giving is an important part of Korean culture, especially for special occasions such as weddings, holidays, or business meetings. When giving a gift, it's important to use both hands and to avoid giving white flowers, which are associated with funerals.

Dining etiquette: When dining with others, it's polite to wait for the oldest or highest-status person to begin eating before starting yourself. Also, it's considered rude to blow your nose or pick your teeth at the table.

Respect for elders: In Korean culture, respect for elders is highly valued. It's important to use polite language and to show deference to older people, especially within the family.

Personal space: Koreans tend to value personal space and may feel uncomfortable with physical contact from strangers. It's important to respect other people's boundaries and avoid invading their personal space.

Group harmony: In Korean culture, group harmony is highly valued, and maintaining a positive relationship with others is considered very important. This means that people tend to avoid confrontation or direct criticism, and may instead use indirect or non-verbal cues to communicate their feelings.

Age hierarchy: Age hierarchy is another important aspect of Korean culture, and older people are typically given more respect and deference than younger people. This means that older people may be addressed with formal titles, such as "ajusshi" (for middle-aged men) or "halmeoni" (for grandmothers).

Punctuality: In Korean culture, punctuality is highly valued, and being on time for appointments or meetings is considered important. If you're going to be late, it's polite to let the other person know as soon as possible.

Drinking culture: Drinking is a common social activity in Korean culture, especially in business settings. It's customary to pour drinks for others and to accept drinks when they're offered. However, it's also important to drink in moderation and to show respect for others.

Modesty: Modesty is considered an important virtue in Korean culture, and people may be hesitant to accept praise or compliments directly. It's also considered impolite to brag or draw attention to oneself.

Importance of education: Education is highly valued in Korean culture, and academic achievement is considered very important. This means that there may be a lot of pressure on students to perform well in school.

Importance of family: Family is also highly valued in Korean culture, and maintaining strong relationships with family members is considered important. This means that there may be a strong sense of obligation to support and care for family members, especially parents and grandparents.

Confucianism: Confucianism has had a profound influence on Korean culture, and its emphasis on hierarchy, respect for authority, and the importance of relationships can be seen in many aspects of Korean life.

Public transportation etiquette: When using public transportation in Korea, it's important to show consideration for others. This means giving up your seat to elderly or disabled passengers, not talking loudly on the phone, and not eating or drinking on the train or bus.

Wedding customs: Weddings in Korea are typically large and elaborate affairs, with many traditions and customs. For example, it's customary for the groom to give a goose or duck to the bride's family as a symbol of fidelity, and for the bride to wear a traditional hanbok dress.

Kimchi: Kimchi is a traditional Korean dish that is made from fermented vegetables, such as cabbage or radish. It's a staple of Korean cuisine and is eaten with almost every meal. It's also considered an important part of Korean cultural identity.

K-pop: K-pop, or Korean pop music, has become popular around the world in recent years. It's known for its catchy tunes, elaborate music videos, and high-energy dance routines. K-pop has become a major part of Korean popular culture and has helped to spread awareness of Korean culture around the world.

Chapter 14: Korean Writing System

The Korean writing system, known as Hangul, was created in the 15th century during the Joseon Dynasty by King Sejong the Great and a group of scholars. Hangul was designed to be a simple and efficient writing system that could be easily learned by the Korean people, who were largely illiterate at the time.

Hangul consists of 24 basic letters, which are consonants and vowels, and can be combined to form syllables. The consonants are arranged in a block shape, and the vowels are written in a line above or below the consonant block.

One of the unique features of Hangul is that it is a phonetic writing system, which means that each letter represents a specific sound in the Korean language. This is in contrast to other writing systems, such as Chinese characters, which are not phonetic.

Hangul is considered to be one of the most scientific and logical writing systems in the world, and it has been praised for its simplicity and ease of use. It has also played a significant role in promoting literacy and education in Korea, as it made it much easier for people to learn how to read and write.

Today, Hangul is the official writing system of South Korea, and it is also used in North Korea and by Korean communities around the world.

Hangul is composed of 14 consonants and 10 vowels. The consonants are pronounced as in English, while the vowels are pronounced differently from English vowels. For example, the vowel "ㅏ" is pronounced as "ah", and the vowel "ㅔ" is pronounced as "eh".

Hangul is written horizontally from left to right, like English. However, it can also be written vertically from top to bottom, as was traditionally done in Korean books.

In addition to the basic letters, there are also "jamo" (diacritical marks) that can be added to modify the pronunciation of a letter. For example, the letter "ㄱ" (g) can be pronounced as either a hard "g" sound or a soft "k" sound, depending on whether a jamo is added to it.

Hangul has been recognized by UNESCO as a Masterpiece of the Oral and Intangible Heritage of Humanity. It is also the only writing system in the world that has a national holiday dedicated to it: Hangul Day, which is celebrated in South Korea on October 9th.

Prior to the creation of Hangul, Korean was written using Chinese characters, which were difficult for most Koreans to learn due to the complexity of the writing system and the fact that Chinese characters do not represent the sounds of the Korean language. The creation of Hangul played a significant role in promoting literacy and education in Korea, and it is credited with helping to spread the use of the Korean language.

Here are some examples of Hangul in action:

- 안녕하세요 (annyeonghaseyo) - This is a common greeting in Korean that means "hello". It is written using six Hangul letters, and each letter represents a distinct sound in the Korean language.
- 한글 (Hangul) - This is the name of the Korean writing system itself. It is written using two Hangul letters: the first letter represents the "h" sound, and the second letter represents the "ah" sound.
- 감사합니다 (gamsahamnida) - This is a polite expression of gratitude in Korean that means "thank you". It is written

using eight Hangul letters, each of which represents a distinct sound in the Korean language.
- 서울 (Seoul) - This is the capital city of South Korea. It is written using two Hangul letters: the first letter represents the "s" sound, and the second letter represents the "uh" sound.
- 삼겹살 (samgyeopsal) - This is a popular Korean dish made from grilled pork belly. It is written using nine Hangul letters, and each letter represents a distinct sound in the Korean language.
- 불고기 (bulgogi) - This is a popular Korean dish made from marinated beef that is grilled or stir-fried. The word "bulgogi" is written using six Hangul letters, and each letter represents a distinct sound in the Korean language.
- 김치 (kimchi) - This is a traditional Korean dish made from fermented vegetables, typically cabbage, and is a staple in Korean cuisine. The word "kimchi" is written using four Hangul letters, and each letter represents a distinct sound in the Korean language.
- 한국 (Hanguk) - This is the Korean word for Korea. It is written using two Hangul letters, and each letter represents a distinct sound in the Korean language.
- 열심히 공부하면 좋은 결과가 있을 거예요 (yeolsimhi gongbuhamyeon joheun gyeolgaga isseul geoyeyo) - This is a Korean sentence that means "If you study hard, you will get good results." The sentence is written using 23 Hangul letters, and each letter represents a distinct sound in the Korean language.
- 동대문 시장 (Dongdaemun Market) - This is a large shopping area in Seoul that is known for its wide variety of goods, including clothing, electronics, and food. The name "Dongdaemun Market" is written using nine Hangul letters, and each letter represents a distinct sound in the Korean language.
- 사랑해 (saranghae) - This is a common phrase in Korean that means "I love you." It is written using six Hangul

letters, and each letter represents a distinct sound in the Korean language.
- 국제공항 (gukjegonghang) - This is the Korean word for "international airport." The word is written using eight Hangul letters, and each letter represents a distinct sound in the Korean language.
- 태극기 (Taegukgi) - This is the Korean word for the national flag of South Korea. The word is written using six Hangul letters, and each letter represents a distinct sound in the Korean language.

Chapter 15: Korean Slang and Colloquialisms

Korean slang and colloquialisms refer to the informal language that is commonly used in everyday conversation among peers and friends in Korea. These words and phrases are not usually found in standard Korean language textbooks and may not be considered proper or formal in many situations. They are often created by combining words, abbreviating words or phrases, or modifying existing words to give them a new meaning or a playful twist.

Slang and colloquialisms are used to add color and humor to everyday conversation and can help people connect and identify with a certain social group or age range. For example, younger people may use different slang than older people, and people from different regions or areas may have their own unique slang and colloquialisms.

It's important to note that while Korean slang and colloquialisms can be fun and useful for everyday conversations, they may not always be appropriate or respectful in formal or professional settings. Therefore, it's important to use discretion and be mindful of the context and audience when using slang or colloquialisms in Korean.

Here are some common Korean slang and colloquialisms:

- 아재판다 (ajae pandah) - Someone who is old and out of touch with current trends and culture.
- 뒷북 (dwitbuk) - Doing or saying something after the moment has passed.
- 꿀잼 (kkuljaem) - Something that is very entertaining or funny.
- 개소리 (gaesori) - Nonsense or BS.

- 헐 (heol) - An exclamation of surprise or shock.
- 짱 (jjang) - Awesome or the best.
- 꽉 잡아 (kkwak jaba) - To hold on tightly, both literally and figuratively.
- 급식충 (geupsikchung) - Someone who is obsessed with school cafeteria food.
- 노답 (nodap) - Hopeless or no solution.
- 대박 (daebak) - Amazing or awesome.
- 멘붕 (menbung) - Mental breakdown or confusion.
- 존버 (jonbeo) - To persist or stick with something.
- 멋쟁이 (meotjaengi) - Someone who is stylish or cool.
- 까불다 (kkabuda) - To criticize or find fault in someone or something.
- 비행 (bihaeng) - Doing something crazy or daring.
- 출근길 (chulgeungil) - The rush hour commute to work.
- 뻥치지마 (ppeongchijima) - Don't lie or exaggerate.
- 말장난 (maljangnan) - Wordplay or pun.
- 야인시대 (yainsidae) - A time of chaos or lawlessness

Again, these slang and colloquialisms may not be appropriate in all situations, so it's important to use discretion when using them in conversation. Additionally, some of these words may have different meanings or nuances depending on the context in which they are used.

www.ingramcontent.com/pod-product-compliance
Lightning Source LLC
Chambersburg PA
CBHW062043290426
44109CB00026B/2717